£5

(790)

GW00361944

THE WOOD
AND THE TREES

AND OTHER POEMS

by

Phillip Clayton-Gore

PENHYDREF PRESS

MMVII

Also by
Phillip Clayton-Gore

Masques from the Mabinogion

First published 2007 by
Penhydref Press
21 Rope Walk, Wellington,
Somerset TA21 9RB

Copyright © Phillip Clayton-Gore 2007

ISBN 978-0-9555103-0-4

A full CIP record for this book is available
from the British Library

Phillip Clayton-Gore has asserted his moral right under
section 77 of the Copyright, Designs and Patents Act 1988
to be identified as the author of these poems.

Printed in the United Kingdom by
Antony Rowe Ltd., Bumper's Farm, Chippenham, Wiltshire
SN14 6LH

*Dedicated to those who have encouraged,
supported and inspired me.*

Phillip Clayton-Gore was born in 1950, in the Gower, south Wales. After a decade in the performing arts, and a decade and a half working at the National Archives, he now lives and works in west Somerset. As well as writing poetry, he is employed as an archivist and administrator, lectures in art history, leads courses in meditation and mythology, and is a member of the Guild of Enamellers.

Some of these poems have previously appeared in other publications, and a number have been presented in public readings and performances. I am deeply grateful to those dear friends who have ushered my work into public awareness on a number of occasions.

CONTENTS

POEMS ALONE

I WILL GO THROUGH THE LAND

I will go through the land that is waking
By highway and track and lane,
And blossom and leaf will be breaking
To welcome me back again;
I will sing to the greening hilltops
And the birds will rejoice with me,
In the Spring that is ever rising
From Oxford to the sea.

I will go through the land that is glorious
By orchard and crop-rich mead,
And flower and fruit will be ripening
With an ecstasy of seed;
I will sing to the fields growing golden
(Though the moonlight paints them pale),
In the Summer that strides forever
From St Bride's to Evesham Vale.

I will go through the land that is weary
By hedgerow and jewelled glade,
Where hips and haws and apples
Are abundantly displayed;
I will sing to the motley woodland
Til echoes pronounce the refrain,
In the Autumn eternally changing
From the Isles to Salisbury Plain.

I will go through the land that is drowsing
By valley and cave and combe,
While a spark that defies the darkness
Ignites in a lightless tomb;
I will sing to the stone-shod dancers
On headland and heath and frore,
For no Winter dozes forever
From Farne to the Severn shore.

I will go through the land and be joyful
By all that there is to be –
Where the land is alive and laughing
And waking along with me;
I will sing of the land that is my land,
And the land will be one with my song,
And the song shall resound through the island –
Blessed and sweet and strong!

THE FLOWERS OF THE NIGHT

Smother all the frantic flames,
And suffocate the light,
And softly call those scented names –
The flowers of the night.

In one dark-petalled cavity
Writhes mystery and might.
Bruise those blooms that none can see –
The flowers of the night.

Sumptuary living shades
Caress and kiss and bite
And feast within these masquerades
On flowers of the night.

The dusty Death's-head plunders
Blind chambers of delight,
And the dark unfolds its wonders
In flowers of the night.

THE MAN IN GREY

Beside the corner
Of my bed
With knowing eyes and nothing said
He stoops and smiles, both glum and gay,
Punctilious Sentinel in Grey.

His pallid skin,
His midnight hair —
His locks too grim, his flesh too fair —
His eyes, where one might drown for aye:
The living Sentinel in Grey.

Two ears attend,
Two eyes appeal,
Long legs that bend so he may kneel
His litanies to softly say,
Strange saviour, Sentinel in Grey.

Pale brow and cheeks
Of moody mirth,
A scent that speaks of silent earth,
A tongue that loves to teach and play:
Unhurried Sentinel in Grey.

His eyes we deem
A moonless night
When lanterns beam the only light —
The Keeper of the Coming Day,
The lordly Sentinel in Grey.

His jaw's well-set,
His gaze is strong,
He'll not forget who does no wrong;
His name no human can betray,
Sardonic Sentinel in Grey.

A brute of beauty,
Free from guile,
With mute and melancholic smile,
And eyes that give the game away,
Beloved Sentinel in Grey.

He shares his sageness
And his grace
With those who assuage his strange embrace.
His unseen store he'll not gainsay
To one who loves
The One in Grey.

THURSDAY AFTERNOON IN THE BRITISH
MUSEUM
for Brian

Prince Khaemwaset, in princely state,
His principal thoughts he would oft relate;
And he uttered such words as could but convince –
"Wisdom = Imagination" said the Prince.

Prince Khaemwaset was young and fair;
The words that he spoke woke the trembling air:
Every scholar that heard has been better since –
"Praise = Knowledge" said the Prince.

Prince Khaemwaset, your words are strong,
And mountains are moved by your princely song:
Such harmonious notes perfect joys evince.
"Truth = Truth" said the thoughtful Prince.

THREE CENTAURS

Three centaurs on the lawn were seen:
They danced a circle round the green;
And, in their dancing, wild and free,
They turned their heads and smiled at me.

Three centaurs on the lawn were seen,
Fleet-footing in a mattachine;
And, in their dancing, wild and free,
They doffed their masks and stamped with glee!

They danced a circle round the green,
Those centaurs sturdy, strong and lean;
They turned their heads and smiled at me
With winks of camaraderie.

In daylight clear, with glorious sheen,
Three centaurs on the lawn were seen –
Such magic in their majesty
And in their dancing wild and free!

They danced a circle round the green
With movements deft and bold and clean;
They turned their heads and smiled at me,
And daylight stuttered suddenly.

And, in their dancing, wild and free,
Was wisdom, wit and grammary;
Three centaurs on the lawn were seen
Where not til now have centaurs been.

With recognition, joyfully
They turned their heads and smiled at me;
By wall of stone and willow screen
They danced a circle round the green.

They, by their boisterous energy
And in their dancing wild and free,
Enchanted my demure demesne –
Three centaurs on the lawn were seen.

They turned their heads and smiled at me,
Accepted hospitality;
They danced a circle round the green
Til evening came and stilled the scene.

They turned their heads and smiled at me;
And, in their dancing, wild and free
They danced a circle round the green.
        Three centaurs on the lawn were seen.

MAUNDY THURSDAY

What new commandment comes our way
On this one loving humble day?

A mandate in an upper room:
A prima vera breaks in bloom.

This new commandment comes to men,
To grind to dust the stony ten.

It speaks to sister and to brother –
"Love one another; love one another."

FLOODED FIELD

The gateway's unobstructed,
The door will quickly yield:
Pass through the mirror-portal
Of the pool in Flooded Field.

Unnumbered feet have trod the road
That wakes the mind new-born,
And yet the living threshold
Is neither hard nor worn.

The changes of the dying day,
The stars' far-distant fires,
Are altered in this smooth dismay
That drowns all small desires.

What worthless shadows will you shed,
What thunders will you wield,
When you stumble through the postern
Of the pool in Flooded Field?

Though Augusts shrink the pond to dust,
They bar the way in vain:
The gate's re-opened in the rush
Of sweet September rain.

The drizzle and the smutchless dew
Diffuse this door unmatched;
And even Winter's icy lock
Is readily unlatched.

While this glassy gate is shifting,
A sword can pierce the shield;
And men and gods may come and go
Through the pool in Flooded Field.

SNOW IN SUMMER

It seldom snows in the Summerlands;
Blizzards are very rare;
Winters seem mild in the Summerlands
When compared with those elsewhere.
North and East may be shrouded white
And drifted deep in snow;
But, though frost may bite, the skies are bright
In the Summerlands I know.

So whence comes snow in the Summerlands?
And when do children stare
At the flustered legions of snowflakes
Crowding the awestruck air?
It is not in mist-wound winter,
Nor in Autumn's weeping gales;
Nor comes the snow marauding
Out of Ireland or of Wales.

But when days wake warm in the Summerlands
And I hear the cuckoo call,
I walk again in the Summerlands
Beside the orchard wall,
Where the blossom is white in the Summerlands
As it breaks on the Summer breeze –
Then it snows, it snows in the Summerlands
From the boughs of the apple trees.

THE CUP

The Cup's never empty, as oft has been shown,
For deep in the Cup is the strength of the Stone;
And the Stone sharpens blades so they pierce like a tooth,
For deep in the Stone lies the Serpent of Truth.

Serpent in the Stone,
Stone in the Cup,
Cup all alone –
Who will sup?

The Cup was kept by a king without a throne,
An ancient of days who understood the Stone;
And the Stone was his joy, and the Serpent he knew,
And he filled the cup with transcendent dew.

The Cup has a secret that some have known,
Who have sipped from the Cup and have kissed the Stone;
And the Stone has blessed their lips and made them strong,
And taught them all the music of the Serpent's song.

The Cup never empties, it never overflows:
It brims with its power, with the wisdom that it knows.
The Stone never fails: it never falls to dust;
It stands in its strength, true to its trust.
The Serpent never sorrows: it is witness to delight,
And transmits the perfect glory of unfailing light.

Stone in the Cup,
Serpent in the Stone:
Who will sup
All alone?

OBERON

Dancing in the dining room,
Or settled in a chair,
Or combing dusky stardust
From the darkness of his hair —
        Oberon, the Faery King,
        Epitome of grace;
        Oberon, the Monarch
        With the moon-bright face.

Sauntering on mazy paths,
Or seated on a stone,
Sovereign of a sylvan host
Who somehow seems alone —
        Oberon, the Faery King
        (What rule to him applies?);
        Oberon, the Monarch
        With the midnight eyes.

Through the shadowed garden
Or beside the ivied wall,
Sometimes clear as crystal
And sometimes not at all —
        Oberon, the Faery King,
        Enchanter of the dance;
        Oberon, the Monarch
        With the might to entrance.

Garbed in glimmered gossamer,
Bejewelled by the dew,
Rover in the moonlit meads
Where Nature greets his crew —
        Oberon, the Faery King,
        Whom no-one can beguile;
        Oberon, the Monarch
        With the star-kissed smile.

KERUX

I am the Warden Deep Within –
The Hound Beyond the Gate
Who keeps, by Aleph, Mem, and Shin,
The Inner Holy State.

Rushing Fire, and yawning Air,
And Water's hummed refrain –
The Mother-letters of the Square,
The Circuit of the Rain.

This is the Magisterial Wand
With Serpents strangely wrought,
That prises open all your minds
To think those things unthought.

This Shining Branch is Hermes' Rod,
With forces unsuspected –
It promises the Truth is odd!
Expect the unexpected!

I shield that perfect occult flower
That flares from seeds divine –
A lamp of blood, a shaft of power,
A silence in the shrine.

I am the Sleepless Watcher
Who sweeps the pathways clean –
The Shadow in the Portal
Unveiling Fires Unseen!

OVER SEVERN IN SPRING
for Eleri

The land of Summer's fair and green
And where I'm pleased to be,
But I know that spring is waking
Across the Severn sea.
So in imagination
I walk through grassy vales
And ascend the mossy mountains
Of my own beloved Wales.

For a daffodil has trumpeted
A clarion-call to me
From the heart that is my homeland
Across the Severn sea.
An all-pervading longing
My senses now assails –
The symphony, the song that is
My own beloved Wales.

I stroll again in Golden Grove
Along by Grongar's lee,
Or gasp at Skomer's splendour
Across the Severn sea;
In Arberth's ring of purple stones
I drink the rain-rich gales,
And the landscape thrums with music
In my own beloved Wales.

The breakers groan at Strumble
On a tide that grieves for me,
And my mind recalls the Mumbles
Across the Severn sea,
For there dwell childhood – endless spring –
And the ancient lovely tales
In that echo of the ages,
My own beloved Wales.

AT THE GROWING ROCK WHERE THE
SWALLOWS GATHER
Gwydion's threnody for Pryderi

Dead Lord of the Circle
Set high above Arberth,
Your brow-star is blinded
And broken your crown;
No more will your triumphs
Re-echo at sunset,
Dead Lord of the Circle,
Dread Lord of Renown.

Fair Lord of the Circle,
Your hair, pale and golden,
Is fallen in ashes,
And lifeless your eyes;
Your flesh and your sinews
Are wasted and shrouded,
Fair Lord of the Circle,
Fierce Lord of Bright Skies.

Bold Lord of the Circle,
Your hills hung with sweetness
Are hoar and untended,
And tainted the wine;
The vintage is spilt
And your cup I have stolen,
Bold Lord of the Circle,
Beloved of mine.

Dead Lord of the Circle,
Be loving and gracious,
Be good to the living
Who dwell here above.
Be greatly forgiving,
Forgive me – who killed you –
Dead Lord of the Circle,
Dear Lord of my love.

ACROSS THE MILES, ACROSS THE YEARS

How many miles to Bethlehem?
The distance is not far –
For Bethlehem still waits for you
Beneath its guiding star.
Its skies still glow with wonder,
Bedecked with lamps above,
Where faith and hope are glimmering
Forevermore in love.

Behold the peace of Bethlehem
Beyond the cheerless roar
Of traffic and the gaudy trade
Of each department store.
Our city streets are crammed with sheep
Who bleat in debt and spite,
But look – above – angelic hosts
Are dancing in the night.

Behold the joy of Bethlehem:
The kneeling ox and ass
That sublimate the tedious spate
Of commerce, coldly crass.
True kings approach with gifts more rare
Than cufflinks, scent and socks;
They doff their crowns and gently smile
And join the ass and ox.

Behold the love of Bethlehem
That echoes down the years –
The love that warms the flowing bowl,
The love that calms all fears;
The love that brings the light again
To lengthen happy days;
The love that drops a silent tear
In wordless, endless praise.

MERLIN, MERLIN

Merlin, Merlin, are you sleeping
Where thorn-blossom still cascades
With Pentecostal blooms a-plenty,
Blanching all the woodland glades
In sweetly-scented shades?

Merlin, magus, are you dancing
On the summer-circled downs?
Are you treading green enchantments
So the streets wear flowered crowns
In our cities and the towns?

Merlin, mazer, leman, lordling,
Blessed service is your spell:
We would lingeringly listen
To the stories you would tell
By the still untainted well.

Merlin, master, are you watching
Moor and mountain, fell and fen,
Standing guard on holy Logres
With a faithful band of men
Til Arthur comes again?
Til Arthur comes again.

DEEDS

I think that at the age of three
A relative remarked to me –
      "You'll never do it. You'll never do it."

And through my youth that litany
Was used to mar my destiny –
      "You'll never do it. You'll never do it."

Then came a curious happening:
I tried and did achieve one thing.
Imagine how, at this event,
My aunts expressed astonishment –
      "Did you do this? Did you do this?"

My mind began considering
A topsy-turvy reasoning:
Perhaps for me to do the deed
There was an odd inherent need
For some unkindly types to say
(Who often do, in just that way) –
      "You'll never do it. You'll never do it."

As I grew up to man from boy,
These twisted words became a joy.
Such sneers appeared designed to bless
And crown me with assured success.
Conviction of a certain winning
Relied on put-downs at beginning –
      "You'll never do it. You'll never do it."

So when idiots with an id to feed
Inveigh against a hatching deed –
Why, then I know I cannot miss:
      I now do this! I now do this!

THE FREEING OF MERLIN

I seem sullen, I seem froward,
And no sane folk speak to me –
For I'm going to waken Merlin
From his prison in the tree.

I have studied subtle quickthorn,
And for long have sought to find
The method to untwine it,
Unlink, unlock, unwind.

I've achieved the nameless hour,
Attained the strength of blood
To force the fruit back into flower,
The blossom to the bud.

Strange words of power will reabsorb
The sapling to the seed;
Its knots will be untangled,
And Merlin shall be freed.

And Merlin shall be freed, and I'll
Announce the fact to men:
That Merlin's free forever –
But what will he do then?

LET ME GO GENTLY
A riposte to Mr. Thomas

Let me go gently into that good night
That is the fate of humankind, the undiverted way,
And – fearless – face the light beyond the light.

Let me be swathed in sentient truth, despite
Antagonists who inwardly their own faint hopes betray;
Let me go gently into that good night.

Let me be strengthened, sensing all aright,
Undazzled by the hurtling stars, or planets where they stray;
And – fearless – face the light beyond the light.

Let me in certainty ride out the night,
Safe-anchored in a harbour that defies the tempest's sway;
Let me go gently into that good night.

Let me, assured, off-cast my shrouding sight
To wake in love, in nakedness that man cannot display,
And – fearless – face the light beyond the light.

Let me not, wretched, writhe – attempting flight
From that embracing angel's shady wings. Nor bid me stay.
Let me go gently into that good night.

Let me not rage, decrepit, wracked with fright,
Nor shy to shut my sun-sick eyes against the fading day.
Let me go gently into that good night
And – fearless – face the light beyond the light.

THE APPLE TREE
for Caitlin

All year round, and starward bound,
All strange events foreseeing,
The Apple Tree, the Apple Tree
Is burning in my being.

When Spring has stirred the sleepers
And the sap begins to rush,
The apple tree is joyful
In the blossom of its blush;
The air is crammed with answers,
And adventuring I go –
I am laughing in the branches
While my sister sings below.

When Summer rouses dragons
And the grain in greenness heaves,
The apple tree is dancing
In the splendour of its leaves;
The day burns long with labour
As I harvest what is made –
I am sweating in the sunshine
While my sister smiles in shade.

All year round, and starward bound,
All strange events foreseeing,
The Apple Tree, the Apple Tree
Is burning in my being.

When Autumn stains the woodland
And the long nights have begun,
The apple tree is heavy
With the treasure of the sun;
The rivers brim with plenty
As I thrash the patient corn –
I go hunting in the moonlight
While my sister sleeps til dawn.

When Winter stills the walkers
And the swallow's safely south,
The apple tree is dreaming,
But its fruit is in my mouth;
The earth has closed its shutters
And I quit the star-fringed shore –
I am kissing in the firelight
While my sister keeps the door.

And all year round, and starward bound,
All strange events foreseeing,
The Apple Tree, the Apple Tree
Is burning in my being.

SATURN IN HIS SEASON
for John

His sombre crown he's keen to quit,
And twit all rhyme and reason:
The old man swanks and skips a bit,
Does Saturn in His Season.

For mumming and for pantomime
He puts his pied chemise on,
To dance those strange days out of time
That Saturn calls His Season.

He jigs and jokes, he laughs and hops –
To say him nay is treason,
Who, gleeful, sows the wealth of Ops:
Great Saturn in his Season!

POEMS FROM EARLIER DAYS

TIME OF LIFE

O please don't pity me, and please don't flatter,
When both my eyes are brimmed with tears and age.
Largesse of yours is sweet, but will not matter
When future tenses vanish from the page.
I'll still write verse, though Time will rudely tatter
The reputation nurtured in this cage.
I'll dream new temples, burning towers of gold,
From shadows in the fire when I am old.

Perhaps when they distilled my cloudy blood,
Some clumsy-footed angel soured the grapes;
I milked my youth in streams that turned to mud
The garden I had planned for Fancy's japes.
And worthlessly I smirked and whiled away
The wasted morning of my wasted day.

APRIL

Soft showers of April gold come spattering
The greenish fields; the half-leaved copses blink
With yellow flowers; brash nettles martyr-ring
The early violets where lovers wink;
The glossy starlings keep on chattering
As hoarse as March – who whistles from his clink
To panting dogs that lie and race and creep
And vie to vex the unity of sheep.

Spring drips like dead-man's grease from Winter's shoes;
The corpse explodes in blossom – white and blush,
Pale amber, purple, cream and azure ooze
In sparkling vintage – herald of the rush
Of Summer's triumphs, trumpets for the clown,
While more resplendent skies invade the town.

SNAP

Last night I came home early
To exercise my lust with someone new.

And so did you.

We stammered a bit;
Let slip embarrassed guffaws;
Scuffed the carpet
(Having ventured an unfortunate step too far).

Eventually we watched those two new people leave
Together.

The irony hardened
In a rigour of unspeaking.

We went to bed
And your back
Warmed my back
Til morning.

And I hated/loved you for it.

FEBRUARY

This is the month Time staggers, sick and lean;
It vomits what remains of Winter's bile.
Slow crunching snow with alabaster sheen
Encroaches indolently mile on mile –
A crusty skin of hoar, a gaberdine
To muffle foison frozen for a while.
These are the days when budding burns to ice,
And frost-brands brown each seedling sacrifice.

Then milder air creeps solemn from the west;
It dries the weeping muzzles of the cows.
A froth of catkins wreaths the month to rest –
Dull golden lambstails dripping from the boughs.
And in neglected graveyards and in dells
The earth with greener fevers gently swells.

MONUMENT

Imprinted on the pavement, shiny wet
In sudden morning sunshine after rain,
A leaf has left its dirty silhouette –
A decomposing shadow in the lane.
One hope of many millions that have set
Memorial reflections to remain
Where others tend their faint posterity,
And weed their graves, and weep in charity.

The sunlight buzzes white along the road,
Imprudently encourages each bud;
The gutter slowly falters, though it flowed
Ten minutes since with mourning tears in flood.
And – though the fancies of the premise stay –
The flagstones dry, the breeze blows dust away.

WHAT WORRIED THE MILLER'S SON

It wasn't the fact
That the cat
Talked.
Or the boots it wore
When it
Walked.
It wasn't the fact
That the cat
Asked him
To take off his clothes
For a swim.
It wasn't the fact
That the cat
In pliant fashion
With consummate ease
Persuaded the giant
To turn into a mouse
That pat
Was trapped.
It wasn't the fact
That the cat
Lapped
The cream off the milk.
None of this disturbed his peace.

But
He sometimes thought he saw
In the cat's skin
A crease.

YESTERDAY'S SUNSHINE

I knew you'd played the game awhile,
I knew you'd been around;
I didn't give a damn for that –
Our love was sure and sound.
We both, without a doubt, could see
Those stars that told us true:
They said that you were meant for me,
As I was meant for you.

Our days were sweetest company,
Our nights one long delight;
Each week sang like a symphony,
Each month shone starry bright.
I held you in my happy arms
And let the kissing start –
A prisoner to your loving charms,
And handcuffed to your heart.

You left behind the merest trace
Of love to shroud despair;
Some cold possessions round the place:
A curly lock of hair,
The shadow of a photograph
(That loving lovely head),
And in my heart your merry laugh –
An echo of the dead.

But that is yesterday's sunshine,
Fragile faded hues,
Stars that have fallen,
History not news.
Yesterday's sunshine,
Last winter's snow,
Gone where
The songs of summer go.

PRISONER

The days are lengthening into my dreams,
Cold as tomorrow, pale as pebbled shores;
The hours stretch the sky's cloud-matted seams,
Horizon-hemmed; and, while the sunset gores
Ill-fitting lives that I have lived, vain schemes
To lighten the darkness and salve all sores,
I count the small divisions of the void
Where fleering youth is greyed and age is boyed,
Degrading respect, debasing each hope.
Year by long year I keep stitching my pall,
As slow as spite and as tight as the rope
Around my neck, til someday I shall fall,
Heedless of ticking, ignoring the chime,
Licking the figures from the face of time.

FOR THE GARDEN

Fate, having done its worst,
Decided to do me a little good one day.
It sent a romantically unclad hero
On a haughty white stallion
Out of my dreams and onto my doorstep.

A randy buck on a dandy steed,
With an amorous finger
He seductively pressed the bellpush.

But I was out.

The horse left
A bucket and a half of manure on the step.

And now I have beautiful roses.

THE MAKING OF THE MIDSUMMER BRIDE
from Four Masques from the Mabinogion

Scatter now throughout the room
Oak and meadowsweet and broom:
   All the ghostly flowers that may
   Be gathered on Midsummer's day.

Flowers of oak and flowers of broom,
Scented meadowsweet in bloom
   Harvested where waters run
   Glimmering in Summer sun.

Lily, in the pool, unblinking;
Campion in long grasses twinkling;
   Budding daisies, day foreseen,
   Beading every dancing green.

Nettles in the dead glades drifting;
Hemlock, hoary umbels lifting;
   Yarrow, blanching meads anew,
   Drenched with tears of Summer dew.

Golden flowers of broom and oak,
Garnered where a sunbeam broke;
   Meadowsweet as pale as prayer,
   Censing all the Summer air.

Bitter strengths of our believing,
Source and cure of human grieving,
   Muster in the waking hour
   When ardent summer aches with power.

Oak and broom and meadowsweet,
Give her grace and dancing feet;
   Make her lovely, loving, mild -
   Flower-Maid, Midsummer's child.

Broom and meadowsweet and oak,
Smiling-voiced and softly-spoke',
                So that Lleu is quite beguiled
                By Flower-Maid, Midsummer's child.

Oak and meadowsweet and broom,
Form her in a dreaming womb:
                "Blodeuwedd" shall her name be styled -
                Flower-Maid, Midsummer's child.

GWYDION'S ENGLYNS TO LLEU
from Four Masques from the Mabinogion

Eagle in the topmost branches,
  Shaded by the open sky,
Do I know you? Will you answer
  When you hear my hopeful cry?

Eagle on the midmost bough,
  In a lordly sanctuary,
If your name is Lleu Llaw Gyffes,
  Loose your talons, fly to me.

Eagle on the lowest perch,
  These arms held wide now welcome thee;
Thus I triumph in my searches -
  Lleu, my lordling, fly to me!

THE INVOCATION TO THE JOURNEY
from In Spæculo Stellorum

Gently, into the darkness,
Launched out of Chaos and Strife,
Over the ocean of matchless Night
Moves the Ship of Life.

The keel is a crescent of silver,
The sail is a nimbus of rain,
And its crew is Love and the brothers of Sleep –
Dreams and Death and Pain.

Softly, breaking the stillness,
A prow that is ploughing the sky,
Trailing uncharted constellations,
The Vessel passes by.

Its wake is a song in the heavens,
Its oars are wings in flight,
And its pitch and roll is a human soul
Surging into light –

Joyful, into the morning;
Joyful, under the Sun;
Joyful and ardent and undeterred,
Our voyage has begun!

O our Ship is a troubled refuge,
Though the Sea is sometimes a friend,
And we deeply grieve for the haven we leave,
Yet we strive for journey's end.

THE MARCH OF THE TREES
from Gwydion

In a season and no season
When the trees were standing still
And the summerfolk were sleeping
Under hedge and holt and hill,
>When the squirrels ceased to prattle,
>Came the summoning to battle,
>And it stirred the restive trees.

In a season and no season
When the trees grew green again
And their leaves produced a clamour
In the turmoil of the rain,
>Up the hill of murder marching
>With their angry branches arching
>Came the armies of the trees.

In a season and no season
When the trees were shedding seed
In a foison which outnumbers
All that human loins could breed,
>Over earth with wild elation,
>Smashing home and habitation,
>Unrelenting, tramped the trees.

In a season and no season
When the trees trod through the sea
In a torrent of true promise
Like a vengeful victory,
>With a surge of fury rising,
>With no hint of compromising
>Strode the regiments of trees.

In a season and no season
When the trees climbed o'er the hill,
Hanging stars upon their branches
And defying winter's chill,

With unlettered imprecations,
Under unknown constellations
Came the unrepentant trees.

In a season and no season
Armoured only with the air,
Guerdoned only with their passion,
All the trees came leafless, bare -
Naked, filled with stubborn folly,
Malice, pride and melancholy,
Came the hosts of wilful trees.

In a season and no season
Ere the battle was begun,
When the fevered moon was bleeding
Like the dying of the sun,
In a dawn bereft of daylight
To a doom bereft of reason,
Mirthless, all the trees came marching
In a season and no season.

GWYDION'S COUPLETS IN ARAWN'S HALL
from Gwydion

All joy, you lords and ladies, be with you in this place.
I hope my rustic courtesy will not evoke disgrace.

Oafish little peasant, with far too short a shirt,
Plaiting birds from flower-stalks, and sitting in the dirt.

Scant of voice and stature, keeping to the wall,
Simpering and shadowless – I'm hardly here at all.

My name is Blood-of-Ashes, unmightiest and least;
A low lout come with open mouth to gawp at Arawn's feast.

THE BARLEY MOW
from The King of Summer

Here's a health to the farmer,
And a health to his men,
And a health to the Barley Mow!
Fat cows in the byre,
Fat sheep in the pen,
And a health to the Barley Mow!
Though the dark days come,
From now til then
Let woeful want
Be far from our ken,
And a health to the Barley Mow!

Good health to the Barley Mow!

Here's a health to the reaper,
And a health to his blade,
And a health to the Barley Mow!
Here's a health to the gleaner,
Be it mother, youth or maid,
And a health to the Barley Mow!
While long summer days
Are loth to fade,
We'll work in the sun
And rest in the shade –
And a health to the Barley Mow!

Good health to the Barley Mow!

Here's a health to the hare
That fled from the field!
And a health to the Barley Mow!
On the threshing floor,
The flail we'll wield!
Good health to the Barley Mow!
May rivalries
Of love be healed!

May our granary
From mice be sealed!
May next year's crop
Be thrice the yield!
And good health to the Barley Mow!
Huzza!
Good health to the Barley Mow!

THE PLAINT OF THE WOUNDED KING
from The Spear

Long are the hours while the sun rules the sky,
And long are the nights with the moon rolling by.
Standing or seated, on my knees or my back,
Half-waking, half-sleeping, while time turns the rack;
Clothed in discomfort and bathed in despair,
Collared by curses that cling to the air.
Long is the night while the sun lets it reign;
Longing am I for its coming again.

Filth in my mouth and dust in my breath,
Longing for healing and longing for death;
Longing for midnight to soothe me at dawn,
Longing at dusk for the bliss of the morn.
Knowing that healing is coming to me,
Aching for knowledge of when that will be;
Livid with pain and living with loss,
Dreaming of crowns and of wounds and the cross.

Blood flows, uncongealing, while life runs awry –
Lord, bring me healing; Love, let me die.

STYX
from The Song of the Styx

I am Daughter of Ocean
And Tethys his Queen;
Conceived in a tempest,
Unkempt and unclean.
Swift in approaching
And slow to depart;
Enraged with the heat
Of the Earth's iron heart.
A turbulent wrath
In an unending flood,
Freezing your reason
And seething your blood.
Splenetic my splendour;
My surge never still;
Undammed my resentment,
My spite and ill-will.

My shallows are deeper
Than you might surmise;
I am bitter to swallow
And burn your blear eyes.
No singer can compass
The scale of my song –
Loveless and kindless
And lightless and strong!
Around Hades' realm
Nine times these floods flow –
A malevolent deluge,
A welter of woe!
On earth, none can match me:
No rapid or strait
Dare vie with this torrent
In permanent spate!

Both Acheron's weeping
And Phlegethon's fire

Evaporate wholly,
Out-faced by my ire.
Cocytos' lamenting
Is stumped to cessation,
O'erwhelmed by the power
Of relentless vexation.
And even chill Lethe
Has shuddered and fled
From the ceaseless abhorrence
That carves out my bed.

ITHACA – I
from Telegonus

Ithaca to my mind always brings
A rocky homeland where a silence sings,
Where a breeze can blow so sharp it scores
The boulders on the spectral shores.

A horseless land – no pasture here –
The hills are steep, the cliffs are sheer;
An isle that's only fit for goats –
On frenzied lazuli it floats.

A gem enduring and adored,
A treasure in a turmoil stored –
Pale flint of brightness in the blue,
All stern directions stem from you!

ITHACA – II
from Telegonus

Little island in the middle,
In the middle of the world,
Like a rocky little riddle
By some giant rudely hurled,
Or a serely beauteous idyll
From the ruffled waves unfurled.

Not a place for trotting horses,
But a perch for agile goats,
Where the tempests run their courses
And the wind its wildness quotes,
While all Nature's ruthless forces
Score a song of thrilling notes.

Isle of stillness at the centre –
Why should any wish to roam?
Welcome waits for those who enter:
Those who breach the booming foam
Join our throng with no dissenter –
O my Ithaca, my home!

Ithaca, my island homeland; Ithaca, my hope, my rest;
Holy barrenness, my heartland, certain target of my quest;
Ithaca, Earth's brightest headland –
Of all isles, one truly blest!

O my Ithaca, the eternal theme
That fires the flame of my soul's one song,
Here I'll wake and work, and here I'll dream
While the winters are weak and the summers are long.

Here the seasons turn, and the honey bee
Stores kisses of gold for my hungry lips,
And the vine that hangs in the olive tree
Bursts in blood-red splendour in each mouth that sips.

At gains I smile, and at losses I weep;
I savour feasts or, steadfast, suffer dearth.
The curt day ends in the arms of sleep,
My flesh and bones return to solemn earth.

Yet when my eyes have guttered and lost their light,
And the fire of my soul's hearth no longer chars,
I shall open my shutters to the boundless night
And, unsleeping, stare beyond the stars.

MERLIN
from The Walker in the Wood

At the hour of my birth I was older than men
And, not wishing to grow any older again,
     I grew younger.
When an infant, observing through eyes that were sage
And charged with the sight that comes only with age,
     I grew younger.
As a schoolboy, untutored by doctor or priest,
But crowned with more nous than a mage of the east,
     I grew younger.
As wiser I grew in search of the truth
That wakes with the anxious recession of youth,
     I grew younger.
As lover unknown, through my own tears I waded;
As soldier I served, and as merchant I traded,
     And grew younger.
Though I thought about rest when old age came to call,
Then I faced the most arduous test of them all,
     And grew younger.
I may seem a sere madman whose manner is wild,
Yet I watch the world wag with the eyes of a child,
     And grow younger,
     Always younger.

BRANWEN'S JIBE
from Four Masques from the Mabinogion

Have you seen a forest
    Of trees upon the sea?
Have you seen the mountain
    That leads their company?
Have you seen on either side the ridge
    Deep pools of light?
And on the summit snow that blazes
    Shadowlessly white?

That forest is a horde of masts,
    Great ships that crowd the sea;
That mountain is my brother Bran
    Who comes in search of me;
Those pools of coldly burning blue
    I know to be his eyes;
Above, his crown has caught the sun,
    And splendour blinds the skies!

Have you seen foul bundles
    Of limbs flung in the sea?
You'll see them, sure, as penance for
    Your faithless treachery!
Have you heard the endless wail
    Of widows for their men?
When Bran arrives, your fearful wives
    Will know the keening then!

My brother, summoned by my wrongs,
    Is coming now with vengeful tread
To tear your poets' lying tongues
    And trample on your nameless dead!

PULVIS ET UMBRA SUMUS
from Into the West

Dust and shadow,
Dust and shadow,
Nothing more than dust and shadow.
Smoke and mirrors,
Lapses, absence,
Figures glimpsed in shifting light;
Pools of silence,
Thickened darkness,
Void of day, and yet not night.

Dust and shadow,
Dust and shadow,
Hush and shapelessness and woe;
Never resting,
Never staying,
Going, or about to go.
Subtle deeps,
Deceptive shallows,
Landscapes into black receding;
Streets untrodden,
Empty closes,
Lanterns in blind alleys bleeding.

Dust and shadow,
Dust and shadow,
Transience and madness meet;
There combining,
There refining,
Wearied triumph, wild defeat.
Nothing more than
Dust and shadow,
Darkness flees where they ignite –
Wake, tomorrow!
Dust and shadow
Exploding in perpetual light!

HOME OF MY HOME
from Out of the West

Home of my home
Beneath the deep waters,
Below the horizon in the woe of the West;
Home of my home,
Your sons and your daughters
Are exiled in sorrow like an unwelcome guest.

Home of my home
Where the drear waves are rolling
In furious stampede or in featureless calm;
Home of my home,
The sad morning's unfolding
On a pitiless ocean, bereft of all balm.

Home of my home,
The sea-birds are calling,
Calling me home to the sea and the sky;
Home of my home
In that endless enthralling,
Doleful and wilful the billows surge by.

Heart of my heart
Where the sun's ever setting,
Far in the West, far under the sea;
Home of my home —
Never forgetting
There, where my heart forever will be.

THE KEEPER OF THE GOLDEN GATES
from Into the West

I stand upon the mountain
That rises from the sea,
And all those sailing westward
Lift hopeful eyes to me.
And I have wished their venturing
The blessing of the Fates –
I, the glassy-armoured guardian
Who keeps the Golden Gates.

Be glad, you sea-sad mariners,
True welcome here awaits
From the crystal-helmed commander
Who keeps the Golden Gates.

The sky is blue above me
When the daystar's clear and bright,
Til it fades to spangled distance
In the sanctuary of night.
The poet utters praises
That my spirit ne'er debates,
As I stand in watchful silence
While I keep the Golden Gates.

Be glad, you sea-sad mariners,
True welcome here awaits
From the crystal-helmed commander
Who keeps the Golden Gates.

You seekers from the sunrise,
Come hither! Here we stay –
A vision in each drowsy heart
That flares at close of day.
Come hither, where the Western Sea
The angry Sun placates.
I call you from the gloaming
Where I keep the Golden Gates.

For when the livid sunset
Accedes to Time's behest,
And with porphyry and purple
Incarnadines the West,
The sea is stained with brilliance
That to darkness dissipates,
And my form stellates the twilight
Where I keep the Golden Gates.

On high, with burning spear and shield,
Above the tireless sea –
A beacon in the dismal dark
That never fails to be.
And earth-born dominations,
Or an emperor's estates,
Are as dust upon my armour
While I keep the Golden Gates.

Be glad, you sea-sad mariners,
True welcome here awaits
From the crystal-helmed commander
Who keeps the Golden Gates.

BLADUD
from Splendor Sulis

I am Untameable Terror,
The Lodestar that burns in the Earth;
I am the Undimming Brightness –
A furnace undamped from my birth.

I am Invincible Burning,
Ruthless and radiant and strong;
Whiteness through redness arising,
Scalding the winds with my song!

From scintillant chasms ascending
To bathe you in mineral dew;
Plundering gems from Earth's mantle,
Your poisons and pain to undo.

I spring to embrace and bring healing:
That is my practical worth –
Through this watery ferment revealing
Love from the core of the Earth.

I am bleached with the rage of the planet,
My hair rises red like a flame,
And my love of mankind is so fervent
I arrive when you whisper my name.

I am such metals as man has not made,
And my foundry's a lonely stellation;
My heart blazes white in the fathomless night –
A fury that fuels Creation!

THE BOAT OF MILLIONS OF YEARS
from Steps in the Dance of Creation

We have taken tall reeds of starlight
And twined them into pliant skeins.

We have plaited strong ropes
From shreds of song –
Like long braids of words,
Inscriptions of truth.

We have bound the gleaming sheaves of rushes
With bands of potent eloquence
Into the shape of a boat

We have drawn lightless pitch
From the fathomless well of night,
And tarred the Boat
With the name of Eternity.

And we sail in the Boat of Millions of Years
On the Unmeasured Tide
Of the Oceans of Time.

We watch the bow of the proud vessel
Cresting the constellations,
And the surge lifts the lotus-prow –
Efflorescent in all collimations.

We hear the lapping of the waves of darkness
Caressing the flanks of the reed-ribbed Boat,
And a song like a bennu bird sounds in the rigging –
Reverberant sweetness in the loud bird's throat.

We smell the spray of the breakers of heaven
And the scent of the burning lamps of the sky.
Our turbulent wake rolls in fragrant devotion
As with untrammelled motion our ship passes by.

We taste the air, the fondling breeze
That fills the belly of the beaded sail.
The strength of song is in our tongues,
And the savour of truth will never fail.

We tread the deck and grip the hawsers,
With ribs of reed beneath our feet;
We feel oars strain, and the vessel swaying,
The assured embrace of each friend we meet.

And we sail in the Boat of Millions of Years
On the Unmeasured Tide
Of the Oceans of Time.

We know of the journey. We speak of the journey.
We know the direction. We speak of the way.
We know of the perils. We speak of the dangers.
We know and we speak of the night and the day.
And we sail in the Boat of Millions of Years
To the shores of Forever,
The harbour sublime.

And we sail in the Boat of Millions of Years
On the Unmeasured Tide
Of the Oceans of Time.

THE SONG OF THE CUMAEAN SYBIL
from The Howl of Night

I am old. I am old.
I am older than most –
Almost older than all,
I heeded the call
Of the Brilliant Behest.
I am oldest of seers,
Seeing better than most
Through the years and the years.
Sensing jeering and jest,
Overcoming the worst,
Outliving the best,
And the years and the years
Are but shadow and dust –
The Might Be, the May Be,
The Shall and the Must.
My choice was to live,
Yet my choosing proved wrong,
And in Time I diminished
To an echoing song.
My fibres of being
Fray and then tear
Til my voice is a fold
In the fabric of air –
And the years and the years
Shall behold me no more
In the vessel of rock
On the star-whitened shore.
I am old. I am old.
And the years and the years
Are unclothed in my oracles,
Washed in my tears.
Scruple and promise
Grow silent and cold
As the Prophetess moans
And grows older than old.
The lees are all gone

And now I must sup
On a breath in the bowl
And a stain in the cup.
I am old beyond measure –
My face disappears;
Flesh and bones fade
In the years and the years.
And the pilgrims attending
To hear me are told
The truth that is truth –
I am old. I am old.

EXTRACTS FROM UNFINISHED WORKS

THE RAMS OF ARES
from Amor and Psyche: the Trouble with Love

We are the rams of Ares –
Whose curly wool is gold –
We feed on iron grasses
And don't require a fold;
We trample all the hedges
With vigorous disdain,
Bronze horns with razor edges –
And very little brain.

We're not Endymion's sheepies,
We're not the lambs of peace,
We are the rams of Ares
Who won't give up their fleece.
You'd best not be believing
That we might well be shorn,
Or else – there's no deceiving –
You'll wish you'd not been born!

We're steel-toothed and malicious,
Not meek or weakly mild
But paranoid and vicious
And violently wild.
Though other sheep are plated
By lanolin alone,
Our wool is lubricated
By pure testosterone!

We are the rams of Ares,
The rams is what we are!
The burly rams of Ares!
Baaa! Baaa! Baaa! *

(* as like a sheep as possible)

EPITHALAMION
from Amor and Psyche: the Trouble with Love

Let Hymen appear in his brightest array,
With fanfares and roses to herald his way;
Let Sun embrace Moon, and let Night embrace Day –
For now is the wedding of Love.
Of Love, of Love,
The wedding of Love!

The mother of Amor has made a decree:
Her son to fair Psyche espoused shall be.
Let Stars kiss the Earth, and let Sky kiss the Sea
Today is the wedding of Love.
Of Love, of Love,
The wedding of Love!

Red poppies have blistered the sheen of the corn:
A droplet of light is the wound he has worn,
But his shoulder of midnight has healed in the dawn
That welcomes the wedding of Love.
Of Love, of Love,
The wedding of Love!

Sweet Psyche has earned all the plaudits of breath:
She has braved all the perils of Beauty and Death,
And echoed the bold proclamation that saith
Today is the wedding of Love.
Of Love, of Love,
The wedding of Love!

Let hearts be in harmony, hand be in glove,
For the butterfly's wings and the song of the dove
Have signalled to Earth and to heaven above
That now is the wedding of Love.
Of Love, of Love,
The wedding of Love!

OUT CAME THE GORGON
from Perseus

Out came the Gorgon!
Brief were the cries
Of those who glimpsed her grief-rimmed eyes.

Out came the Gorgon!
No curse or moan
Was made by those first turned to stone.

Out came the Gorgon!
Men stumbled to their doom,
Fleeing, eyes shut, from the petrified room.

Out came the Gorgon!
And the hero's sword clove
The heads from the hoodwinked who desperately strove
To escape from the Gorgon,
To avoid her dismal gaze,
Through the wide well-lit hall that was now a lightless maze.

In the stare of the Gorgon
They tripped across each other,
And some yelled worthless orisons,
And some wailed "Help me, brother!"

High he held the Gorgon,
The hero tall –
High, triumphant, deadly – as he strode around the hall.

He came at last with the Gorgon
To the king on his stink-soaked bed
Where the monarch had shrouded his raiment
About his trembling head,
Had wound it there so tightly,
In such a close embrace,
That the weave's untroubled pattern
Was impressed upon his face.

First one arm, then the other,
The hero chopped, hooked clear;
The helming robe was rent to show
The king's eyes shut in fear.
Then, with a ruthless surgeon's skill,
Obstructions to excise,
Perseus slit the king's eyelids –
And eyes met eyes.

The sobbing king, in dying saw
The Gorgon's endless gaze,
And froze in that chill unsensing
That gods cannot erase.

Slow moments grew to minutes,
Til Perseus stood alone
In a crowd of witless statues
In a court of stone.

Back went the Gorgon
To the darkness of the sack,
Where her sightless eyes burned blankly
In a cavity of black.

TENEBROSO
from An Angel Passes

Darkness, into your embrace
My yearning soul must fall.
Light has scarred my woeful eyes,
So while the day in silence dies
I listen for your call.

Darkness, be my all in all,
Submerge my mind in sleep.
Now, as brilliant hours depart,
Whisper to my weary heart,
Wrap me in your deep.

Darkness, in your realm you keep
Strange raptures deemed unknown.
Seekers for these secrets fare
By sea and strand and mountain where
Nameless winds have blown.

Darkness, claim me as your own;
My star grows dimly old.
Lift me in your lightless arms
And furl me in unflustered charms
While your tale is told.

Darkness, hasten to enfold
My eyes, my brow, my face.
Smoor my beaming consciousness,
Inflamed with teeming fear and stress;
Bathe me in your grace.

All I am, in love I place,
Darkness, into your embrace.

THE WOOD AND THE TREES
A poem in nine parts

I – Faunus

Beyond the reach of the smooth-faced road,
Over the moss-browed stile,
Into the shade of the living wood
Our steps will lead for a while.

And each leaf-featured face
And each bark-skinned sprite
Will greet us in the Greenwood,
In the thin green light.

My hooves have been shiny
In the melting snow,
And my hairy limbs have shivered
While the cold winds blow,
But the year's awake and dancing
In the swift-advancing Spring
Where the daffodils are trumpeting
And cowslip-bells ring.

The snowdrop and the crocus
Have announced drear days departing,
And pussy willow's budding
Where the warbler's deftly darting.
The grasses seize the sodden earth
And grow with sudden vigour,
Rejecting all the sullenness
Of Winter's woeful rigour.

Arise! The world has wonders,
But none fairer that I know
Than the living lovely Greenwood
Where you and I will go.

Do not rush, do not hurry,
Do not race along the track;
No need to run or scurry,
Nor scramble to get back.

Be as timely as the trees,
Slow the urgency of blood
Til it matches in its movement
The heartbeat of the wood.

Then your being may be listening
To the aged ageless song,
And your voice may join the music
That your heart knew all along.

This is the way through the woodland;
This is the way through the woods.

No lane is lost in the woodland,
For the forest holds in its earth
Centuries of seasons –
Of plenty and of dearth.

Weather and rain ne'er undo it;
It seeds all its greenness anew;
And it holds in its infinite wonder
The secrets of leaf-fall and dew.

II – The Voices of the Dryads

Listen – We speak for the wood in all seasons.
Our words are sung in the fluttering of leaves,
Or written in naked branches scratching the indifferent sky.

True spirits of the living trees
That hold communion with the breeze,
We share our sorrows and our mirth
With light and moisture, air and earth.

Our flame is a greenness.
The wind holds our wonder,
And the earth our thirsty secrets.

III – The Turning of the Year

There is an insistent whisper of Spring in the wood –
A breath of verdure unfurls in astonished blossom
And blood-rich leaves.

Now comes the face of the Sun,
Scrubbed, shaven, newly washed,
Into the open-eyed Spring.
Liverish Winter, wrinkled and discoloured,
Crazes, cracks, and new growth emerges.
Vibrant skies tumble into the incredulous woods.

Laughter echoes in the gossiping glades.
Infants stir in the widening days.

Osier greening on the brook's brown bank,
Swaying in the mirror of the wind-stirred stream,
Cupping in branches that are blistering with leaf
The watery orb of the Spring Sun's gleam.

Birch, first greener of the dancers in the wood,
Daintily feathered with the trophies of Spring,
Spurting like a fountain in the spark of morning,
Whispering a triumph where the small birds sing.

Cob, green giver of the bounty of the woodland,
Rayed like a star in the coppice and the grove,
Generous provider in an early season –
Wisdom is the jewel in your treasure trove.

The song of the season
Is in the breezy mornings
And the showery afternoons.

The incision of Spring
Uncoffers greenness
In grass and leaf,
And whistle and beating wing
Greet a cleanness
That fleeces grief.

See, the Moon rises, increscent,
From the belly of the setting Sun,
And a sliver of silver
Sheds its soft gleam in the west.

Now comes the gaudy triumph of the year,
And the labour of the woodland
Works green wonders in the world.

Thorn, when the green and the white come together,
Snow in early summer, scenting every breeze,
Creating gems of redness in your secret dreaming,
Garlanding the lovers in the lush green leaze.

Ash, rising green to the stroke of heaven,
Dancing to the echo of the storm-browed Sun,
Defiant, courting danger in the awestruck meadow,
While the pale-shirted reapers cast their scythes and run.

Oak, growing greener in the shining Summer,
Sovereign of vast acres of auriferous grain,
Steading of the eagle in the midst of harvest,
Scattering cupped acorns in your wide domain.

The song of the season
Is in the somnolent midday
And the languorous imprecision of dusk.

Green, green summer
In a green, green shade –
Hill-crowning hanger
Or hidden glade.

Time seems to stammer
Where in warmth is laid
A wonder and a splendour
That is unafraid –
Unheeding of the moment
That is here and gone,
Unknowing that the summer
Is over and done.

See, the plenitude of the Moon
Comes close to the Earth,
Anointing the parched fields.
With the fullness of harvest.

Now come the painted players
On embroidered gales of shimmering rain,
Hurtling from the branches
To seek the thinning warmth
Of Autumn's earth.

Apple, bleeding Summer in your blushing greenness,
Diseased by dropping sweetness and debauched by duty;
You have fed the honey-brewers in the blossomtide
And yield us the succulence of toothsome beauty.

Beech, your greening fruit has blanched with ripeness
And is uttered from your branches to attentive ground,
Where dribbling maws of many will devour your children
To fatten for the Winter whither all are bound.

Elm, softly coffered in green mould and mosses,
Stately and unbending, with your saw-toothed leaves,
And your bole, burred and burly, your branches ascending
Into grey billowed blusters where your torn crown heaves.

The song of the season
Is in the reiving of the evening wind
And in the imprisoning drizzle as the nights draw in.
Reddened over-ripeness

Seceding to decay;
Brashly painted faces,
Brittle with dismay –
Livid on the branches,
Bearded on the ground,
Blossoming grey-greenness
Unwholesome and unsound.

In coloured earths these shattered leaves
Their loveliness rescind:
Oracles of yesteryear,
Dust upon the wind,
Echoes crowding wooded aisles,
Elements unmade,
Faint shadows of a tree that falls
Within a noiseless glade.

The harvest topples homeward,
The fruit draws near my lips;
The last fond bee from laggard blooms
With anxious longing sips.
And silent Winter stillness
Engenders in the night
Ten million tiny daggers
In a massacre of white.

See, the Moon turns her face and departs –
A shadow in the star-pierced sky;
And the trees are hung with subtler jewels
In the glimmer of darkness.

Now comes the silence, shattered by axes;
And trees are felled to quell the hunger of the season.

Holly, first of evergreens that star the woodland,
Armoured with a shimmering and sharp array,
Sentinel of Summer in the dark plantation,
Berried with the redness of expiring day.

Ivy, winding greenness through the wordless forest,
Caressing blushless stones with your many-handed arms;
Flowered with geometers, fruited with intoxicates,
Sealing wounds of sorrow under shadow-woven charms.

Yew, green and shrouded in the white-cloaked season,
Guardian of the ages on your stone-ringed hill;
Sleep and death are as moments in your thinking,
Seeming silent, waiting long, and dreaming still.

The song of the season
Is in the midnight's unspoken hour
And in the red-eyed rime of reluctant dawn.

Now, through the branches bare
The thin flakes fall;
The huddled woodland starts to wear
A thin white shawl.
The ground is wet and chill with woe,
And draws a coverlet of snow
Across faint paths where few feet go –
And no birds call.

Grey the clouds above the hill,
The fear-blanched crest
Where Winter, with a callous will,
In frost is dressed.
The ground's unyielding to the eye
Of Sun that, sullen, passes by,
Deep-mantled in the loveless sky
And feeble still.

Grey the ice that rims the stream
As day fast dies;
Bleak the Moon's half-shuttered beam
To weary eyes.
The trees are naked in the night,
Victims of the Winter's spite –
Blackness withered by a white

That petrifies.

Now, through the branches bare
The thin flakes bring
A heaviness that clogs the air,
An uttering
That smothers in a silent flood
The leaf-mould, moss and filmy mud,
And stifles the imprudent bud
That longs for Spring.

I am burning, I am burning
In the night that seems unending –
I am burning on your hearthstones
For the unborn and the old;
Raging through the winter darkness,
With my life your lives defending;
Blazing as in battle
Against the deathly cold.

And, in slumber, slumber turning
Ere the Year begins to rove,
Comes a knowing, yielding, yearning
In the Silent Grove.

IV – The Silent Grove

No sound, but the river flowing by.
No sound, but Sun and Moon burning in the sky.
No sound, but the wind riding the weather.
No sound, but the earth abiding alone and altogether.
      No sound, in the Silent Grove.

No sound, but the root drinking.
No sound, but the leaf breathing.
No sound, but nectar brimming in the cup of the flower.
No sound, but the seed hardening in potency.
      No sound, in the Silent Grove.

No sound, but a taste familiar and beguiling.
No sound, but a vision smiling.
No sound, but a scent of below and above.
No sound, but a touch of love.

V – Hymn to Pan

In all seasons, one turning.
In all turnings, the Wood and the Trees.
In the Wood and the Trees, Pan.

Piper in the mist-wreathed morn, you
Prance among the woodland shades;
Horns of dream and dread adorn you,
Keeper of the green-lawned glades.
Early, ere the stars are drowned;
Late, when day has blushed and died,
Comes a cloven footfall's sound –
An outward fear, a joy inside.

Loving, frantic, living God,
Perfect trembling, blissful terror,
Green and goodly, mirthful, odd,
Strange musician, free from error,
Wildness whistling in the blood,
Hurtling through our hastening hearts,
Freedom that is understood
By the panic it imparts.

Dissolve the thoughts that chain the mind;
Release the heart incarcerate;
With your truth, the gut unbind;
With your passion, liberate!
Wake us to your clarity;
Break the world's o'erweening power;
Bring us to eternity
In the wisdom of your hour.

VI

In the crevices of bark,
On the pitted face of stones,
In the mould and in the dark
Dwell the beings without bones.

And the lichens and the mosses
Make their microscopic spinneys
Where the foxglove dreams and dosses,
Where the horse-fly rears and whinnies.

No stranger than the miniature,
The woodland too is weird.
Imagination seems unsure
On ways unnamed, un-steered.

Here, all seems strange – a fiction
Where the trees are speaking, dancing:
Deportment mixed with diction –
Exuberant, entrancing.

Lavishness, luxuriance
In Summer's sumptuous haze;
Echoes and endurance
Through Winter's hueless days.

Look – the tree-tops court the lightning.
Earth shivers at the thunder,
As the Wisdom of the Wildwood
Is unwound in fear and wonder.

Know the progress of the instant,
Know the wisdom that is rife,
Know the pageant of the Seasons –
The metonym of Life.

VII – The Dryads speak again

We are singularities in a multitudinous existence.

Time is longer here.
We regard the turning of a year
As but a single day in the witness of our world.
Time is sweeter here.
We expect seasons in due course,
Like meals and recurrent events in your diurnal round.

Time is lovelier here.
Song and silence come one and another
To enrich the minute that you would term a day.
Time is evenly paced here.
We have no sense of boredom
In our evolving existence.

Time speaks more softly here.
Day and night are but tick and tock
In the multitude of beats that mark a year.
Time tastes stranger here.
The instant of the mayfly's life
Is unremarked in the millennia of the oldest trees.

Time hears nothing here.
Even our music is less than the briefest reverberation
In the symphony of All That Is.
Time touches here.
All that is moves on, unfurling, unfolding,
Augmenting the skeletal leaf-litter
That blows among the stars.

VIII

And All That Is is here, now.
And All That Is is always.
All is growing and yet not increasing.

Matter transforms.
Time unwinds.

We shall not be here for ever.
The witness of our being shall echo
In a morning-song;
And other worlds shall wake to the curious chance
Of the Wood
And the Trees.

IX – Faunus speaks again

I have heard, under dry leaves of Autumn,
Small animals forage for food,
Or deep in the half-smothered burrow
A somnolence slowing the blood.

I have seen in the bareness of Winter,
Sad hunters in desperate mood
Scratching the skin of the woodland,
Searching for something of good.

I have smelled in the triumph of Springtime
The birth-scent surrounding each brood,
And in the drowned brooks and the ditches
The decay of the fever-month's flood

I have walked in the wide days of Summer
Through the woodland that wears a green hood,
Where all living beings are busy
In the legion that fashions the Wood.

The world is a turning of torment –
But the Wood can offer some ease,
For the Wood is not merely the moment,
The Wood is not merely the Trees.

IMAGINATION

You tell me there's a lot you know,
And put stored evidence on show –
It's true you know a lot, but oh
       What do you imagine?

Your facts are plain, we all admit;
Your information lacks no whit;
But when all's said and done with it,
       What do you imagine?

If I require some dismal truth
Regarding someone's broken tooth,
You'll know it – yet, in serious sooth,
       What do you imagine?

A dreamer has a mind so wide
That galaxies can grow inside –
Is this a universe untried?
       What do you imagine?

THE LAST OF SUMMER

One last Summer day
Though the swallows have flown
And the long nights their shadows impose,
One last Summer day
In the green Summer lanes,
And the smile of one last Summer rose.

RAGGED ANGELS

Past disregarded dangers
On a path of dedication
I pursue the ragged angels
Of my wry imagination;
To the detriment of duties
And the clock's unheeded preaching,
I follow rugged beauties
Ranging freely, teasing, teaching.

Present weighty obligations
Burden every step and pacing;
Only hard-breathed profanations
Overtake the ones I'm chasing.
Yet they still dance on before me,
Loving, living, giving, guiding,
Whilst I curse my earthbound torment
And I crave their fond abiding.

Future splendours break the shadow,
Deftly stringing me along
With the promise of tomorrow
And the wholeness of a song.
I still stumble on the stairway,
I still stutter, tongue and tooth.
But the truth I seek is beauty,
And that beauty is my truth.

AIDONEUS

Purple shadows stain the sky;
The silhouetted trees
Are blackness and the sombre leaves
Are silent in the breeze.
Unseen, with perfect mastery
You tread the mossy maze,
And penetrate the twilight
With your dark-eyed gaze.

Bloodless roses crown the thorns,
Bone-white in the bud;
Distantly there comes the moan
Of streams in loveless flood.
The half-light brims with sorrow,
Regrets suffuse the haze;
Impassive, you observe all
With your dark-eyed gaze.

Lightless robes adorn your shape,
Encase your blushless form
In sovereign anguished midnight –
The mantle of the storm;
The pure deeds of your justice
Upon your pale brows blaze,
And the essence of your power resides
Within your dark-eyed gaze.

WILL YOU?

Will you read my words when I am dead,
And wonder what I knew of laws or lovers?
Or will you leave my woeful words unsaid,
And never prise apart these printed covers?

This language may have passed and been forgotten,
Reclassified as some barbaric tongue –
Will you decide to chant things ill-begotten,
Refuse to leave these syllables unsung?

And if you make a vaulted chamber tremble
By speaking potent phrases from my pen,
Will listeners in attentive ranks assemble
To try to comprehend my verses then?

Read, if you will, my words when I am dead,
And let them echo on the artless air.
If they engender joy or love or dread,
Dispersed in dust, I'll neither know nor care.

Published in a limited edition of 100, of which this is number .71.....

*